M000159658

JESS CONTE

day by day

100 WAYS TO CAPTURE MEMORIES AND CREATE YOUR OWN STORY

A GUIDED JOURNAL

Ellie Claire
gift & paper expressions

...inspired by life

DEDICATION

To my family, my team, and my amazing husband—
for always inspiring me and encouraging me toward my dreams.
I love you all so much!

And to every person who loves journaling as much as I do.

THIS BOOK BELONGS TO:

Breaish Blaylock

DATE I STARTED THIS JOURNAL:

06/28/2023 ☀

DATE I COMPLETED THIS JOURNAL:

/ /

INTRODUCTION

Welcome to the *Day by Day Guided Journal*! Whether you're new to the world of journaling or, like me, you've always been drawn to putting pen to paper, I'm so glad you're here.

I actually can't remember a time before I was keeping a diary or a journal of some sort. There's a good chance I was barely old enough to be writing in complete sentences when I began filling up those first pages. But what I do know is that the two main reasons I fell in love with journaling as a child are still the reasons I love it today, and why I wanted to create this experience for others.

CAPTURING YOUR STORY

With every journal entry—no matter the length or whether the topic is silly or serious or even seems mundane—you are taking a written snapshot of a specific time in your life. All together, those recorded moments can become the stories of our lives for us and others to look back on.

When I was around twelve years old, I created a journal with my lifelong best friend (whose name also happens to be Jess). We've always lived at least a few hours away from each other, so each time we reunited we would write in this journal—me always with red ink and her always with blue. We would write about what was trending at that time, the latest phone (throwback to the Motorola Razor), favorite songs of the moment...or really anything. We got a kick out of recording anything that was going on in our lives or in the world around us. That journal became our very own time capsule. And it's filled with some of my favorite memories to look back on.

Now, over a decade later, I still enjoy writing down the current things that are happening, heavy things on my heart, or simply what I am up to each day. I love the thought of my future kids reading the entries when they're my age and seeing how different life was. And also seeing how some things never change—like our need for love, kindness, and self-acceptance, and that choosing gratefulness (especially for the little things) just makes life better. There's space in this journal for you to capture it all.

MAKING THE MOST OF "ME TIME"

Even when I haven't consciously been aware of it, writing things out has been a consistent way I take care of myself, from the inside out. If there's something that's really on my heart, writing about it helps lift that weight off my shoulders. But self-care through journaling doesn't always have to look like heavy-duty self-reflection.

There are times when we just need to keep it light. I've found that coloring pages and other creative activities can offer just as much enjoyment and comfort as an adult as they did when I was a kid. Creating lets my brain shift gears, relax, and release the intense parts of life a little bit. And maybe this is revealing a little Type A in my personality, but if you're like me, sometimes it just feels really good to make a list. *Any* kind of list—from the day's to-dos to future goals to your dream road-trip itinerary. Listing helps me pull that endless swirl of thoughts out of my brain and create a little space to just be.

Whatever the day, whatever your mood, I want this book to be a place where you can pop in and get the peace, rest, or release you need in a given moment. That's why—right along-side prompts that help you process, reflect, and record—I've filled this journal with lots of opportunities to sketch, color, create, and play. A mini escape where you can set aside the stresses of the day as you immerse yourself in the pages. A place to put down your phone for a few moments and pick up a pen instead.

Let these pages serve as a quiet way to start your morning, a relaxing way to end your night, or simply a way to make the most of any time at all. Because quality time is a gift we also need to give to *ourselves*. And I hope this journal can help you do just that.

HOW TO USE THIS JOURNAL

GO AT YOUR OWN PACE.

Maybe you're someone who likes to journal at a set time every day and gets satisfaction from filling out every page in order. That's great—the way this book's activities and prompts are organized will keep you engaged and interested with variety and color.

Or maybe you're more of an on-a-whim journaler. Perhaps you'd like to pick up wherever you left off whenever inspiration (or the need to process life a bit) strikes. That's perfect too. By incorporating four different themes throughout, this journal is designed to *meet you wherever you're at* in a given day or moment. And while the order of the prompts may feel random at first glance, they are intentionally so.

It doesn't matter if you complete this journal in a few months or if it takes you a couple of years of hopping in here and there. Let the opportunities this journal provides give you time to slow down for a moment and enrich your life in your own way, in your own rhythm.

CHOOSE A THEME THAT FITS YOUR MOOD AT THE MOMENT.

Every new day is different, and our needs for a creative outlet differ accordingly. That's why there are four different types of activities to choose from. And because every category has its own color stripe at the top of each page, you'll be able to quickly and easily thumb through the journal and find the type of activity or prompt that feels right or most enjoyable to you at the time.

CHECK-IN Daily (or anytime) opportunities to briefly document your day, choose gratitude, and tap into a little self-care. Whatever your routine, these entries offer regular moments of quiet reflection and mini resets for your mind, body, and heart when you need them.

CAPTURE A variety of fun prompts for exploring and recording your life at this moment in time. From lighthearted polls to favorites lists to fill-in-the-blank "my life" trivia, your answers will add up to your own colorful me-myself-and-I time capsule.

CREATE   Artful activities to engage your creative side. Put on some good music and relax as you work on inspirational coloring pages or make a themed photo collage. Whether you need a little art therapy or just the simple pleasure that creating can bring, these pages are just the ticket.

REFLECT + GROW   Thoughtful questions for self-discovery plus activities and ideas for becoming your best and healthiest self from the inside out. Reflect on your history, imagine your future, and become more aware of what makes you tick and what makes you *you*. Whether you're setting new goals or examining old habits, let these prompts keep you inspired on the journey toward the life you want to live and the person you want to become.

IT'S YOUR PERSONAL TIME. MAKE THE MOST OF IT.

There are no rules to this journal, but I do have a few encouragements for getting the most out of using it:

1. When journaling, leave your phone in another room or change your settings to "do not disturb" so you can really breathe deep, relax, and soak up the moment.

2. Be free to be completely honest with yourself, even if an answer feels awkward. It's *your* journal—let it be true to you.

3. Have fun!

I can't wait to see what you discover as you explore your own mind, heart, and life experiences through journaling. Snap a photo of the prompts or activities you most enjoyed and share them with me! #daybydayjournal

Now go enjoy some quality *Me Time*.

EVERY DAY MAY NOT BE GOOD,
BUT THERE'S SOMETHING
GOOD IN EVERY DAY.

alice rose earl

GOALS

////////////////////////////

If you aim at nothing, you'll hit it every time.

ZIG ZIGLAR

What a great quote! Not only setting goals, but making them more concrete by actually writing them down, is a great way to hold yourself accountable for the things you want to achieve.

While big goals might be the most fun to think about, I've found that sometimes it's the smaller goals that make a greater impact on my daily life. One of my current small-scale goals is to meal prep every Sunday, setting Gabriel and myself up to be able to have healthy lunches and dinners during the busy week. My "dream big" goals include renovating a house and traveling throughout Europe. So much adventure ahead.

List any goals you have, whether they're small and easy to achieve or more big-picture life goals, along with an action that will get you one step closer to completing each one. Circle or color in the icon that best represents the scale of each goal (from highly aspirational to doable in the near future) to identify which goals you should be prioritizing and working on first.

KEY: ☁ dream big ☆ work hard ⅄ small steps

SCALE	GOAL	TO GET ONE STEP CLOSER
☁☆⅄		
☁☆⅄		
☁☆⅄		
☁☆⅄		
☁☆⅄		

26

dream big ☆ work hard Y small steps

SCALE	GOAL	TO GET ONE STEP CLOSER
☁ ☆ Y		
☁ ☆ Y		
☁ ☆ Y		
☁ ☆ Y		
☁ ☆ Y		
☁ ☆		
☁ ☆		
☁ ☆		
☁ ☆ ☆		
☁ ☆		
☁ ☆ Y		
☁ ☆ Y		
☁ ☆ Y		
☁ ☆ Y		
☁ ☆ Y		
☁ ☆ Y		

Se
Seas
Holida
Animal.
Social m
Beauty pr
Emoji (draw

Share your ans

27

THE START OF SOMETHING NEW

Cue the song from *High School Musical*. This space is for anything that you wouldn't quite put on your #Goals page but would still like to try. What are you curious about? What sounds fun, but you've never let yourself go for it? It could really be anything: "make a new recipe," "go one day without social media," "try in-line skating," or "take a pottery class." The more—and the more uniquely you—the better! Keep exploring. It's what keeps life interesting.

Share your answers on social media! #daybydayjournal

DATE	NEW THING	✓	DATE COMPLETED

DATE	NEW THING	✓	DATE COMPLETED

SELF CHECK-IN: BODY

//

Our bodies work so hard to take care of us. Let's take a quick pause to think about how we can better take care of them today too. Before answering the following questions, take a few slow, deep breaths.

Date: _____

Physically, I feel _____ today.

Does any part of my body hurt or ache?

YES   (circle one)   **NO**

If yes, what? _____

One thing I can do to care for my body today (e.g., stretch,

go for a walk, get a massage, make a green smoothie, etc.):

_____

Have I had enough water so far today? (Circle)

YES, I'm on track!   **NO, I'll drink a glass right now.**

My stress level right now is at a (circle):

0   1   2   3   4   5   6   7   8   9   10

What activities will I do to release stress from my body today?

_____

_____

What's something I can do today to set myself up for a good night's sleep later on?

_____

_____

Other than the above, how was my day?

_____

_____

31

THINGS TO CHECK OUT

It's hard for me to narrow down movies and books to my favorites (I love almost any rom-com movie and almost any mystery novel!), but here are a few of my favorites in other categories:

TV shows: *Monk, The Blacklist, The Office, Parks and Recreation*
Artists: Ed Sheeran, Lauv, Justin Bieber, Sasha Sloan
Podcasts: *Crime Junkie*

Do you ever hear someone talking about a movie or podcast they thought was amazing, but you can never remember what it was when you actually want to watch or listen to something new?

Write it down here. You'll know right where to go whenever you're ready to check out something highly recommended in the near future.

MOVIES

_____

_____

_____

_____

_____

_____

TV SHOWS

_____

_____

_____

_____

_____

_____

BOOKS

_____

_____

_____

_____

_____

_____

SONGS/ARTISTS

_____

_____

_____

_____

_____

_____

PODCASTS

_____

_____

_____

_____

_____

OTHER

_____

_____

_____

_____

_____

MY REVIEWS

//

Rate the latest restaurant, coffee shop, hair salon, book, movie, etc., you've tried lately, and create your own 5-star review system. It's a fun way to capture memories (even experiences that deserve a terrible review sometimes make the funniest memories later), and everybody loves a great recommendation from someone they trust. Feel free to snap a photo and share your recs with friends. *(And don't forget to color in the stars for your 1- to 5-star rating!)*

What: _____	What: _____	What: _____
Review: _____	Review: _____	Review: _____
_____	_____	_____
Rating: ☆☆☆☆☆	Rating: ☆☆☆☆☆	Rating: ☆☆☆☆☆

What: _____	What: _____	What: _____
Review: _____	Review: _____	Review: _____
_____	_____	_____
Rating: ☆☆☆☆☆	Rating: ☆☆☆☆☆	Rating: ☆☆☆☆☆

What: _____	What: _____	What: _____
Review: _____	Review: _____	Review: _____
_____	_____	_____
Rating: ☆☆☆☆☆	Rating: ☆☆☆☆☆	Rating: ☆☆☆☆☆

What: _____	What: _____	What: _____
Review: _____	Review: _____	Review: _____
_____	_____	_____
Rating: ☆☆☆☆☆	Rating: ☆☆☆☆☆	Rating: ☆☆☆☆☆

YES I CAN
YES I CAN
YES I CAN

SELF CHECK-IN: HEART

Our emotions are external messengers for what's going on within. It's always worth the time to stop and listen to what they have to tell us and examine where we might need to give ourselves a little more TLC today.

Date: _____

In this moment, I feel _____ .

So far, the high point of today has been:

_____

So far, the low point of today has been:

_____

Something that has been on my heart recently:

_____

Something I can do to feel more at peace or give myself space today:

_____

Someone I want to reach out to/connect with today:

_____

At the moment, something I'm learning about myself is:

_____

Other things on my heart:

_____

_____

_____

_____

I think the "little things" are a big part of what makes life beautiful, especially when we take the time to appreciate them. Here are some of the simple things that I find delightful:

- a good cup of tea
- a rainy day spent at home, on the couch with a blanket
- farmer's markets
- fresh flowers
- the feeling you have after a great hangout session with family or friends
- traveling to a new place
- coffee shop date
- the smell and feel of a new book
- a clean home
- Christmas Eve
- a new planner

On the lines, map out twenty little things that light you up inside. Even better, see how many of them you can fit into this week!

DECOMPRESS & DRAW

To be honest, drawing is not one of my strengths. But I don't let that stop me from using it as an outlet to relax or create for no other purpose than the pleasure of it. And I hope you won't either. There is something so life-giving about turning off the logic side of your brain and just making art, however simply or imperfectly.

Put on some good music, an audiobook, or a podcast you enjoy and let your mind unwind as you draw shapes or doodle freely. This experience is not about what appears on the page; it's about the inspiration and relaxation that comes when you let yourself create without rules or expectations. Just draw and enjoy!

MY FAMILY
//

Family, to me, is my husband, my parents, my brother and sister, and my pup. Together, they are my sense of home and comfort.

Family. What's so beautiful about that word is that it means something different to everyone. For some, family includes a parent (or parents) and siblings, grandparents, aunts, uncles, and cousins. For others, it is the community around them and the friends they surround themselves with. Whatever family looks like or means to you, share it here.

A portrait of my family (draw or tape photos here):

NAME:
RELATION:
AGE:
ONE WORD TO DESCRIBE THEM:
MY FAVORITE THING ABOUT THEM:

NAME:
RELATION:
AGE:
ONE WORD TO DESCRIBE THEM:
MY FAVORITE THING ABOUT THEM:

NAME:
RELATION:
AGE:
ONE WORD TO DESCRIBE THEM:
MY FAVORITE THING ABOUT THEM:

NAME:
RELATION:
AGE:
ONE WORD TO DESCRIBE THEM:
MY FAVORITE THING ABOUT THEM:

NAME:
RELATION:
AGE:
ONE WORD TO DESCRIBE THEM:
MY FAVORITE THING ABOUT THEM:

NAME:
RELATION:
AGE:
ONE WORD TO DESCRIBE THEM:
MY FAVORITE THING ABOUT THEM:

NAME:
RELATION:
AGE:
ONE WORD TO DESCRIBE THEM:
MY FAVORITE THING ABOUT THEM:

NAME:
RELATION:
AGE:
ONE WORD TO DESCRIBE THEM:
MY FAVORITE THING ABOUT THEM:

Favorite memory with my family:

_____

_____

_____

_____

_____

_____

_____

_____

_____

_____

_____

FRIENDS I'LL NEVER FORGET

Whether we know them for a season or for our entire lives, our friendships grow us, stretch us, comfort us, make us laugh, and ultimately change our lives. Identify which of your friends fits each description below and write down a memory you have of them that you'll never forget.

Friend who kept my secrets: _____

Memory: _____

Friend who was my opposite: _____

Memory: _____

Friend who got me into trouble: _____

Memory: _____

Friend I've known the longest: _____

Memory: _____

Friend I miss the most: _____

Memory: _____

Friend who was the most creative: _____

Memory: _____

Friend who brought out my competitive side: _____

Memory: _____

Friend who saw me through one of my hardest seasons: _____

Memory: _____

SELF CHECK-IN: MIND

///

Our minds are the hub for our overall well-being. Take a few minutes for a little mental check-in.

Date: _____

Right now my mind feels (circle): clear / fuzzy / tired / buzzing / calm / overwhelmed

What I'm most looking forward to today: _____

What I'm most worried about right now: _____

Biggest items on my to-do list today:

☐ _____

☐ _____

☐ _____

What I need to let go of/release control of: _____

One thing I can do to nourish my mind today: _____

One thing I can do to rest today: _____

Other things on my mind: _____

_____

_____

_____

_____

_____

_____

_____

WHAT WOULD YOU DO IF YOU KNEW YOU COULD NOT FAIL?

There's a little trick I've found that helps me whenever fear of failure is holding me back from something I want to do. I ask myself, "What is the worst-case scenario that could happen if I do this?" and then "Will I survive it?" The answer to the second question is almost always yes. And, here's the thing: Even if the outcome isn't what I wanted, I've never regretted showing up for myself and just going for it—whatever that looks like. And you won't either.

Make a list of what you would do if you knew you could not fail—and then make a plan to do it!

_____

_____

_____

_____

_____

_____

_____

_____

_____

_____

_____

_____

_____

_____

_____

_____

_____

_____

_____

WHERE I'VE BEEN

Color in the map where you have been in the world.

MY TRAVEL BUCKET LIST

As you list your dream destinations, keep in mind that a trip doesn't have to be pricey or take you halfway around the world to be memorable. There may be amazing locations that you've yet to explore that are closer to home.

My current travel Bucket List:

☐ _____
☐ _____
☐ _____
☐ _____
☐ _____
☐ _____
☐ _____
☐ _____

Somewhere I'd like to go to again:

_____

If I could learn another language, it would be:

_____

My best travel buddy:

_____

My ultimate road-trip snack list:

☐ _____
☐ _____
☐ _____
☐ _____
☐ _____

TODAY WILL BE A GOOD DAY.

SELF CHECK-IN: BODY

//

Our bodies work so hard to take care of us. Let's take a quick pause to think about how we can better take care of them today too. Before answering the following questions, take a few slow, deep breaths.

Date: _____

Physically, I feel _____ today.

Does any part of my body hurt or ache?

YES   (circle one)   NO

If yes, what? _____

One thing I can do to care for my body today (e.g., stretch,

go for a walk, get a massage, make a green smoothie, etc.):

_____

Have I had enough water so far today? (Circle)

YES, I'm on track!   NO, I'll drink a glass right now.

My stress level right now is at a (circle):

0   1   2   3   4   5   6   7   8   9   10

What activities will I do to release stress from my body today?

_____

_____

What's something I can do today to set myself up for a good night's sleep later on?

_____

_____

Other than the above, how was my day?

_____

_____

WRITE ABOUT A TIME WHEN YOU EXPERIENCED PURE HAPPINESS.

It's interesting how some of the sweetest moments in life can happen despite—or even because of—something difficult. When I married my American husband, Gabriel, and we moved to the United States, I had no idea it would be two and a half years—due to US residency paperwork challenges—before I would be able to return home to Australia. It was my first time to move away from home, much less halfway around the world, and I was so homesick to see my family. When I got the news that the process was complete and I could finally fly home for a visit, it was one of the happiest moments ever. I asked my sister to help keep our arrival a surprise for my parents and brother. They had no idea we were coming. When Gabriel and I walked in the door, the look on their faces and the way we all felt is something I'll never forget.

One of the beautiful things about writing out a truly happy moment is that you get to relive the joy of it all over again. I hope it fills you up.

_____

_____

_____

_____

_____

_____

_____

_____

_____

_____

_____

_____

_____

_____

A *brain dump* is exactly what it sounds like—a place to empty your head when it's too crowded with thoughts, ideas, questions, or worries. Use this space to gain clarity or simply put a thought down someplace where you won't lose it. Come back anytime you need a little less mental distraction and a little more peace of mind. (PS: You'll find more space to empty your mind onto paper on page 120.)

BRAIN DUMP

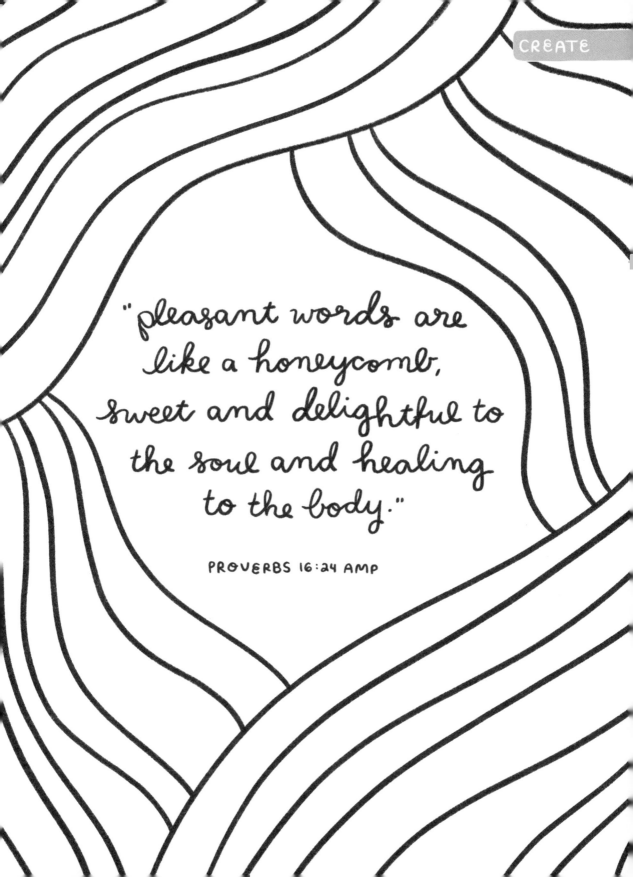

"pleasant words are like a honeycomb, sweet and delightful to the soul and healing to the body."

PROVERBS 16:24 AMP

SOCIAL MEDIA DETOX

///

I really enjoy social media and think there is so much good that can come from it. (I actually met my husband because of it!) But I also found that being able to see what people are posting and commenting at any point of every day was not good for my mental health. I also didn't like the thought of being addicted to it, and how sometimes—without even realizing it—my thumbs would unlock my phone, swipe straight to a social media app, and all of a sudden I was scrolling. How did I get here?!

So, a couple of years ago, I made a goal to take one day off social media each month. And by the end of my first detox day, I didn't even miss being on it. I thought I would be afraid I was missing out all day, but it actually felt so refreshing to not know what everyone was doing at every moment of the day. Even after just twenty-four hours away from social media, I felt more invested in what really matters to me in real life. I hope you'll find the same is true for you!

At its best, social media is an incredible tool for connecting us to new information and inspiring ideas, reconnecting us with old friends, and introducing us to a lot of new friends. But it can also be a pretty negative space. Think about it: When you watch a TV show episode or a movie there is a defined ending, but there's no end to a social media feed. We can keep scrolling forever, and in the meantime, lose touch with the tangible world around us.

A periodic social media detox day can be really helpful to keep strong boundaries and a healthy balance between the virtual world and the real world.

If you're an avid social media user, taking a whole day off might sound difficult. But the key to a great social media detox day—where you're not constantly reaching for your phone or accidentally opening an app—is to have engaging activities already planned. And the benefits will be so worthwhile!

Here are some detox-day activity ideas to get you started:

- Paint by number
- Journal
- Have a picnic with friends or family
- Walk your dog
- Browse a bookstore and start a new read
- Work out
- Create your own spa day with skincare products and face masks
- Bake some treats and share with family and friends
- Take a bubble bath
- Play a board game
- Do a puzzle
- Clean your home/bedroom
- Watch a movie

my social media detox day plan

I'm going to take a social media detox day on: _____ (date)

What apps I'm not going to use: _____

_____

Tip: Try keeping your social media apps in one folder on your phone. The night before your detox day, move the app folder to a new page on your phone (somewhere your thumbs won't automatically/unconsciously swipe to)!

Instead of getting on social media, this is what my day will look like:

_____

_____

_____

_____

I've taken a social media detox day (circle one):

    Never

    Once or twice before

    A lot! I love it!

I think this will be (circle one):

    So easy! I don't get on social media very much.

    Fun! I'm excited to spend some time off social media.

    A little challenging, but something I want to try.

    Difficult...but I'm excited to see how it goes!

Share your answers on social media with the hashtag #daybydayjournal (before your detox day!) to hold yourself accountable and encourage others to take some time off their phones too.

SELF CHECK-IN: HEART

Our emotions are external messengers for what's going on within. It's always worth the time to stop and listen to what they have to tell us and examine where we might need to give ourselves a little more TLC today.

Date: _____

In this moment, I feel _____ .

So far, the high point of today has been:

_____

So far, the low point of today has been:

_____

Something that has been on my heart recently:

_____

Something I can do to feel more at peace or give myself space today:

_____

Someone I want to reach out to/connect with today:

_____

At the moment, something I'm learning about myself is:

_____

Other things on my heart:

_____

_____

_____

_____

1- YELLOW 2- LIGHT BLUE 3- CREAM/WHITE
4- DARK GRAY 5- LIGHT GRAY 6- RED/PINK 7- DARK BROWN

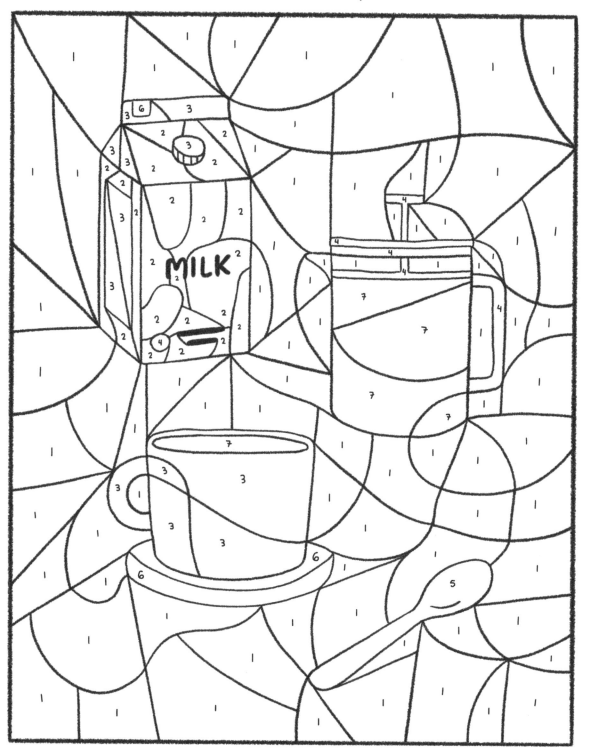

WRITE A LETTER TO: SOMEONE WHO HAS GREATLY
INSPIRED YOU OR INFLUENCED YOUR LIFE.

You know those sayings like "you become the five people you hang around the most"? Well, I sure hope that's true, because the person I hang around the most is also the person I most deeply admire: my husband, Gabriel. His faith, his charisma, his work ethic, his drive and discipline, his kindness and heart for people—it has been so special to witness all of it up close over these years we've been together. Knowing him has made me a better person. I'm so grateful to be spending my life with someone who lives in such a way that pushes me to grow every day.

Picture the person whose life has had the greatest influence or impact on your own. What would you tell them about your life now? How did their care shape you or your path? How has their example or their investment in your life made you a better person?

Dear: _____

_____

_____

_____

_____

_____

_____

_____

_____

_____

_____

_____

_____

_____

_____

_____

_____

_____

_____

_____

_____

FIXING YOUR SLEEP SCHEDULE

///

I've always been more of a morning person than a night person. In fact, 9:30 PM is usually my threshold for socializing before I get tired and start shutting down. (I know, I'm a bit of a wild one.) Still, whether it's been because of traveling, working late, or hanging out too late, I've definitely had my fair share of irregular sleep schedules. But I'm one of those people who really needs eight hours of sleep a night to function well and feel healthy. So when I feel my sleep pattern getting off, I go back to these simple practices to help me get back on track.

As you read through the tips below, think through your own sleep habits. What small adjustments to your bedtime routine might help move you toward the best and most rested version of yourself the next morning?

Tips for how to get a full, good night's sleep:

- Work your way up to your goal of total sleep time *incrementally*—even simply getting to bed fifteen minutes earlier than the day before is a great shift toward your ultimate goal.
- Put away your phone an hour or two before going to sleep. Give your eyes and mind time to unwind from looking at a screen.
- Don't keep your phone on your nightstand or right next to your bed when you go to sleep. Instead, put it across the room or, even better, in another part of the house. That way, you won't be distracted by notifications or sucked into scrolling through social media right before sleep.
- Get a real alarm clock instead of using your phone for your morning alarm, eliminating the need to keep your phone beside your bed.
- Allow yourself a realistic "wind down" time. Try giving yourself at least fifteen to thirty minutes of quiet downtime in bed before sleep.
- Read a book, journal, pray—anything that doesn't include a screen—before going to sleep, allowing your brain to relax and get sleepy in a more natural way.

my sleep schedule plan

On average, what time do you go to sleep right now? ___ : ___ AM / PM

What would be your ideal time to wake up? ___ : ___ AM / PM

How many hours of sleep do you want/need to have each night? ___ hours

How much time do you want to give yourself to wind down/get sleepy? ___ minutes / hours

What are some goals that you're going to set in order to get a good, full night's sleep? (Check those that apply.)

☐ Put phone away ___ minutes / hours before going to bed.

☐ Not have my phone next to my bed but somewhere else in my room / house.

☐ Not look at my phone for the first ___ minutes / hours after I wake up.

☐ Read / journal before going to sleep.

☐ Other:

Come back and report! How did it go?

_____

_____

_____

_____

_____

_____

_____

SELF CHECK-IN: MIND
//

Our minds are the hub for our overall well-being. Take a few minutes for a little mental check-in.

Date: _____

Right now my mind feels (circle): clear / fuzzy / tired / buzzing / calm / overwhelmed

What I'm most looking forward to today: _____

What I'm most worried about right now: _____

Biggest items on my to-do list today:

☐ _____

☐ _____

☐ _____

What I need to let go of/release control of: _____

One thing I can do to nourish my mind today: _____

One thing I can do to rest today: _____

Other things on my mind: _____

_____

_____

_____

_____

_____

_____

_____

What are some of the experiences you don't want to miss out on in your lifetime? Nothing is too big or small!

Some items from my own Bucket List:

1. *travel throughout Europe*

2. *renovate a house*

3. *learn another language*

4. *learn how to make pottery*

5. *become a mother*

6. *learn sign language*

7. *attend a US sports game*

8. *release my own music*

9. *plant my own veggie garden*

MY LIFE BUCKET LIST

1. _____
2. _____
3. _____
4. _____
5. _____
6. _____
7. _____
8. _____
9. _____
10. _____
11. _____
12. _____
13. _____
14. _____
15. _____
16. _____
17. _____
18. _____
19. _____
20. _____
21. _____
22. _____
23. _____
24. _____
25. _____
26. _____
27. _____
28. _____
29. _____
30. _____

Share your Bucket List on social media! #daybydayjournal

THIS OR THAT: FOOD

If you *had* to pick...

Breakfast	Dinner
Tea	Coffee
Pizza	Pasta
Waffles	Pancakes
Salty	Sweet
Nutella	Peanut Butter
Chocolate	Vanilla
Takeout	Home-Cooked
Fruits	Vegetables
Ice Cream	Frozen Yogurt
Sparkling Water	Still Water
Candy	Chocolate
Apple Juice	Orange Juice
Mild	Spicy
Milk Chocolate	Dark Chocolate
Toast	Cereal
Cookie	Brownie
Fruit Smoothie	Green Juice
Glazed Donut	Jam-Filled Donut
Peanut Butter & Jelly	Ham & Cheese

TIME TO RECHARGE

///

Whenever I've taken personality tests, the results have always been mixed. Turns out I'm pretty close to a 50/50 introvert/extrovert, and that feels pretty accurate. I find that I'm more extroverted around introverted people, and I'm more introverted around extroverted people. Go figure! I do love alone time, though. Sometimes all I need is a day at home by myself just organizing the house, cooking, or simply lying on the couch with a movie and my pup beside me. I really do love hanging out with people, but I find that if I go too long without some quality alone time, I start to feel really drained. But if I listen to the cues my body gives me—those signals that I'm overwhelmed or stressed—I can hit pause and create some space to recharge by myself. And when it's time to work with or hang out with people again, I can truly enjoy them and have something to give.

When your body and mind are running on empty, do you notice in time to refuel without a crash? Take a few minutes to think through what you need in order to recharge.

I consider myself an: (a) Introvert (b) Extrovert (c) Something in between.

Explain: _____

_____

After a long day, I'd rather: (a) Go out and see my friends (b) Have a night in by myself.

How I can tell my internal batteries are running low: _____

_____

Top-three simple pleasures:

1 _____

2 _____

3 _____

A place that is restorative for me: _____

_____

Activities that help me recharge when I'm feeling drained: _____

_____

_____

MAKE A PLAN:

What's something simple you can do to reenergize yourself?

- Today:

_____

- This week:

_____

_____

- Anytime/at a moment's notice:

_____

_____

What kind of personal retreat would you like to go on someday? Where? When?

_____

_____

What does it look like when you have a healthy balance between work and leisure time or between your social life and time alone? What does that feel like?

_____

_____

"YOU DON'T NEED TO TAKE ALL THE STEPS, JUST THE NEXT ONE."

bob goff

SELF CHECK-IN: BODY

//

Our bodies work so hard to take care of us. Let's take a quick pause to think about how we can better take care of them today too. Before answering the following questions, take a few slow, deep breaths.

Date: _____

Physically, I feel _____ today.

Does any part of my body hurt or ache?

YES   (circle one)   NO

If yes, what? _____

One thing I can do to care for my body today (e.g., stretch,

go for a walk, get a massage, make a green smoothie, etc.):

_____

Have I had enough water so far today? (Circle)

YES, I'm on track!   NO, I'll drink a glass right now.

My stress level right now is at a (circle):

0   1   2   3   4   5   6   7   8   9   10

What activities will I do to release stress from my body today?

_____

_____

What's something I can do today to set myself up for a good night's sleep later on?

_____

_____

Other than the above, how was my day?

_____

_____

COMMUNICATE & CONNECT

Whenever someone asks me for a piece of advice on relationships, whether it's with a friend, partner, or family member, the first thing I always say is "work on your communication."

Good communication is the thread that connects us to those we care about most. It's how we strengthen relationships and have meaningful moments of connection in our lives. What are your favorite ways and settings to give and receive good communication?

Favorite way to communicate with people in my life (circle):

(a) Text (b) Call (c) Video call (d) Letter

Other: _____

I like when people in my life reach out to me through (circle):

(a) Text (b) Call (c) Video call (d) Letter

Other: _____

Best way to get to know a new friend (circle):

(a) Meet for lunch (b) Invite them over (c) Attend an event together

Other: _____

Preferred way to "talk it out" or have a difficult conversation (circle):

(a) Over the phone (b) Meet for coffee (c) Go on a walk together

Other: _____

Favorite way to spend quality time with family (circle):

(a) Play a card or board game (b) Get outside together (c) Cook together

Other: _____

Favorite way to spend quality time with a friend (circle):

(a) Coffee date (b) Video call catchup (c) In PJs on the couch (d) Picnic

Other: _____

My favorite thing to talk about with my:

Parents: _____

Spouse or significant other: _____

Sibling: _____

Best friend: _____

Coworker: _____

What are some ways I want to grow in becoming a better communicator?

_____

_____

What is one thing on my heart right now that I need to communicate to someone?

_____

_____

_____

MY DREAM DAY

- - - - - - - - - - --- -- - - - - - --- -- - - - - - - --- -.

My dream day would look like waking up before sunrise (after a full night's sleep!), hiking for a great view of the sunrise with friends, and going out for breakfast afterward. Then I'd get a facial or a couple's massage with Gabriel—something super relaxing. I'd end the day with dinner and a game night with family and friends. Just a simple, fun-filled day with the people I love.

If you could plan a day to do *whatever* you wanted *whenever* you wanted—free from any responsibilities for twenty-four hours—what would it look like?

I'd wake up at:

___ ___ : ___ ___ AM / PM

With an alarm   (circle one)   Without an alarm

What I would do:

MORNING:

_____

_____

AFTERNOON:

_____

_____

EVENING:

_____

_____

My meals:

Breakfast: _____

Lunch: _____

Dinner: _____

I would go to sleep at:

___ ___ : ___ ___ AM / PM

MY VISION BOARD

//

When we are able to really visualize what we want our lives to be like, we're that much more likely to make it happen. Making a vision board can help bring your goals and dreams into focus in a creative way, and it's easy to do.

1. Search magazines (or sites like Pinterest) for images, words, and phrases that align with your vision for the next season of your life. Maybe you want to spend more time outdoors. Maybe you want to start cooking more. Maybe you want more quality time with loved ones.

2. Cut out photos and words that symbolize these aspirations.

3. Create a collage by gluing them onto the following pages.

   Tip to stay inspired: Take a photo of the vision board you created and make it your phone background to keep your goals in sight.

   Here's a vision board I made for myself:

Share your vision board on social media! #daybydayjournal

SELF CHECK-IN: HEART

Our emotions are external messengers for what's going on within. It's always worth the time to stop and listen to what they have to tell us and examine where we might need to give ourselves a little more TLC today.

Date: _____

In this moment, I feel _____ .

So far, the high point of today has been:

_____

So far, the low point of today has been:

_____

Something that has been on my heart recently:

_____

Something I can do to feel more at peace or give myself space today:

_____

Someone I want to reach out to/connect with today:

_____

At the moment, something I'm learning about myself is:

_____

Other things on my heart:

_____

_____

_____

_____

HABIT TRACKER

We know it takes lots of repetition to create good habits, but how often do we actually track the habits we're trying to establish so we can visualize our progress? A habit tracker is a great way to hold yourself accountable for your goals, to show your progress, or just to help keep you on *track* with your week.

Choose one thing you want to focus on over the next month. List that goal at the top of one of the charts below, and each day that you accomplish it, come back and color in the coordinating square for that day. Maybe you've been exhausted lately and a Sleep Tracker would be helpful for making sure you're getting eight hours of sleep more often. However you utilize these monthly trackers, their purpose is to bring awareness and help motivate you toward creating habits that make your life better, *not* to make you feel bad for what you're *not* doing. Any single square that you fill in is a victory!

Examples of habits to track:
- Workouts
- Reading
- Prayer
- Cooking at home
- Waking up before a certain time
- Falling asleep by a certain time
- Practicing a hobby
- Filling out this journal! :)

GOAL: _____   MONTH & YEAR: _____

MON	TUE	WED	THURS	FRI	SAT	SUN

GOAL: _____   MONTH & YEAR: _____

MON	TUE	WED	THURS	FRI	SAT	SUN

GOAL: _____   MONTH & YEAR: _____

MON	TUE	WED	THURS	FRI	SAT	SUN

THIS OR THAT: WOULD YOU RATHER...

Circle your preference. If you *had* to choose, would you rather...

Be able to fly	Be invisible
Go back in time	Go into the future
Be a famous actor	Be a famous singer
Be able to speak to animals	Be able to speak every human language
Have more time	Have more money
Have a rewind button	Have a pause button
Always be too hot	Always be too cold
Have a time machine	Be able to teleport
Have bad breath	Have smelly feet
Have eyes that can film everything	Have ears that can record everything
Have a dog with a cat's personality	Have a cat with a dog's personality
Spend a day with your favorite book character	Spend a day with your favorite movie character
Take a rocket to Mars	Scuba dive to the deepest part of the ocean
Be late	Be early
Spend the rest of your life on the beach	Spend the rest of your life in the mountains
Be the smartest person in the room	Be the funniest person in the room
Get stuck in a broken elevator	Get stuck on a broken-down gondola
Be able to breathe underwater	Be able to walk through walls
Be a fabulous cook	Be an amazing athlete
Arrive to a party overdressed	Arrive to a party underdressed

IS THERE SOMETHING YOU NEED TO LET GO OF? OR SOMEONE YOU NEED TO FORGIVE?

I don't think forgiving necessarily means forgetting (or else I probably wouldn't believe in the value of journaling so much). But I do believe that all of our experiences, especially the painful ones, shape us. And when I've chosen to forgive someone or let go of a negative experience, I've been shaped for the better. I've grown. And I've become more of the person I want to be.

Choosing forgiveness is not easy. And sometimes the hardest person to forgive is myself. It's so easy to beat myself up about things in the past, but now I try to let it be a reminder of how much I've grown since. We are constantly evolving, and making mistakes is going to be part of that journey. Offering yourself forgiveness is so necessary to live a life that is healthy, whole, and generous. I want to be all those things, and I want that for you too.

Whatever you need to let go of or whomever you need to forgive, let go of that weight to-day as you put it down on paper. Write a letter to someone you need to forgive (even if that's yourself). It doesn't need to go anywhere outside of these pages. And you'll feel a whole lot better after you do.

_____

_____

_____

_____

_____

_____

_____

_____

_____

_____

_____

_____

SELF CHECK-IN: MIND

///

Our minds are the hub for our overall well-being. Take a few minutes for a little mental check-in.

Date: _____

Right now my mind feels (circle): clear / fuzzy / tired / buzzing / calm / overwhelmed

What I'm most looking forward to today: _____

What I'm most worried about right now: _____

Biggest items on my to-do list today:

☐ _____

☐ _____

☐ _____

What I need to let go of/release control of: _____

One thing I can do to nourish my mind today: _____

One thing I can do to rest today: _____

Other things on my mind: _____

_____

_____

_____

_____

_____

_____

MY CURRENT PLAYLIST

I love acoustic music, chill pop, and worship music. I find that I tend to listen to more music that I can sing along to.

What do you have *on repeat* lately? Create a playlist of your current favorite songs. Fill in the titles and artists below. And if you're feeling artsy, draw or print out and glue the song artwork in the spaces below.

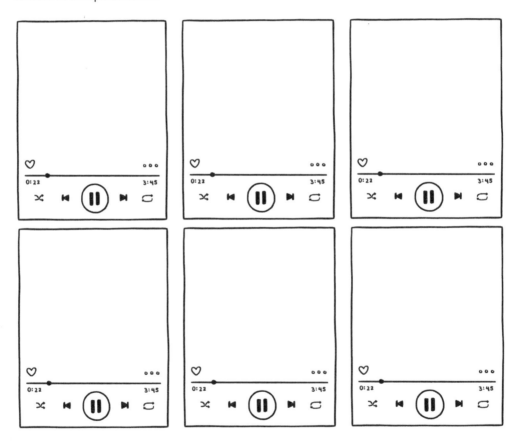

When you look at your completed playlist, would you say it's an accurate soundtrack of your life right now? Circle:

yes!

this is basically my
life as a musical

no

I just love the vibes

MOMENTS THAT MAKE ME SMILE

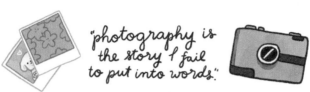

"photography is the story I fail to put into words."

DESTIN SPARKS

Create a photo collage of your favorite memories. Use double-sided tape to stick on printed photos. Write the year and memory next to each image.

"whatever you are,
be a good one."

ABRAHAM LINCOLN

SELF CHECK-IN: BODY

//

Our bodies work so hard to take care of us. Let's take a quick pause to think about how we can better take care of them today too. Before answering the following questions, take a few slow, deep breaths.

Date: _____

Physically, I feel _____ today.

Does any part of my body hurt or ache?

YES   (circle one)   NO

If yes, what? _____

One thing I can do to care for my body today (e.g., stretch,

go for a walk, get a massage, make a green smoothie, etc.):

_____

Have I had enough water so far today? (Circle)

YES, I'm on track!   NO, I'll drink a glass right now.

My stress level right now is at a (circle):

0 1 2 3 4 5 6 7 8 9 10

What activities will I do to release stress from my body today?

_____

_____

What's something I can do today to set myself up for a good night's sleep later on?

_____

_____

Other than the above, how was my day?

_____

_____

FILL IN THE BLANKS: WHAT MAKES ME... ME

Complete the sentences and create a little snapshot of some of the things that make you uniquely *you*.

I can't leave the house without _____ .

I don't feel normal unless I _____ .

It makes me laugh when _____ .

I can't stand it when _____ .

I wish that _____ .

I'm my goofiest self around _____ .

If I had to eat one food every day, it would be _____ .

My most used phrase is probably _____ .

My favorite way to greet a friend is _____ .

I'm usually awkward when _____ .

Something I'd like to work on is _____ .

I don't understand how people don't like _____ .

I feel old when _____ .

I feel young when _____ .

My best-kept secret is _____ .

I can't go to sleep if _____ .

Share your answers on social media! #daybydayjournal

MY CHILDHOOD

Place a photo here of yourself as a child.

It's funny how when you start reminiscing about life when you were a kid, your mind goes immediately back in time to experience it all over again. Use these questions to capture a bit of your childhood.

What do you know about the day you were born? Day, time, any details of what happened?

_____

_____

What is your earliest memory? _____

_____

What was your nickname? _____

Where did you grow up? City life or country life? _____

_____

Who lived in your home? (Mom? Dad? Siblings?) _____

_____

Did you have any pets? _____

Did you have any chores? _____

What was your favorite home-cooked meal? _____

_____

Did you play any sports or any instruments? _____

Who was your favorite teacher? _____

What was your favorite subject in school? _____

What did you want to be when you grew up? _____

What was your favorite TV show or movie? _____

Who was your favorite musician/artist? _____

Who was your best friend? _____

What adult in your life did you most admire when you were a child? _____

What was your favorite hobby? _____

What were you afraid of? _____

What were you good at? _____

Did you have a funny email address? (*Note from Jess:* Mine was groovygirl...yikes!)

_____

WRITE A LETTER TO: YOUR YOUNGER SELF

When I look back at my life, there are lots of things I would love to tell my younger self. Things like:

Soak up the time you have with your best friends. Once you graduate, it's harder to see those people as you get different jobs and different schedules, and people move to different towns (or countries!). Treasure the season you're in where you get to see them at school every day!

There are going to be some people who are mean for no reason other than jealousy or their own unhappiness. Just know that your worth is not defined by their opinions of you.

Pursue your faith even when you feel alone in it. It gets a little harder when you move away from what you're familiar with, but keep seeking it out. It is your anchor.

It's okay not to know what you want to do when you graduate from high school. Just continue to pursue your hobbies and passions, and you will eventually figure it out.

It doesn't matter if you haven't had your first kiss by the time everyone else has. It doesn't make you any less cool or worthy.

Continue making those silly, funny videos with your friends...the editing practice will pay off one day.

Writing a letter to a younger you is a great opportunity to channel some self-love and self-compassion, get a better understanding of yourself, and maybe even gain some closure. What did you spend time worrying about that eventually turned out fine? For what are you proud of yourself? What's one piece of advice you wish you'd been given? Tell yourself what you wish you had been told by someone else back then.

Dear _____ -Year-Old Me,

_____

_____

_____

_____

_____

_____

_____

_____

_____

_____

_____

_____

_____

_____

_____

_____

_____

_____

_____

_____

_____

_____

_____

NOTICING DETAIL

Even a few moments outside can do so much for your body, mind, and heart. Grab a pencil and—whether you put down a blanket in the yard, find a park bench, or drive to a remote spot outside of town—find a place to sit and notice the world around you.

Pick one small object to look at closely (e.g., a leaf, a stick, a stone, etc.). Notice the tiny veins in the leaf, the texture of the bark, or the lines in the rock. Sketch what you see below.

SELF CHECK-IN: HEART

Our emotions are external messengers for what's going on within. It's always worth the time to stop and listen to what they have to tell us and examine where we might need to give ourselves a little more TLC today.

Date: _____

In this moment, I feel _____ .

So far, the high point of today has been:

_____

So far, the low point of today has been:

_____

Something that has been on my heart recently:

_____

Something I can do to feel more at peace or give myself space today:

_____

Someone I want to reach out to/connect with today:

_____

At the moment, something I'm learning about myself is:

_____

Other things on my heart:

_____

_____

_____

_____

CREATE

patience is bitter
but its fruit is sweet

aristotle

ON MY PHONE...

The type of phone I have: _____

My most-used app: _____

I prefer to (circle):   (a) Text   (b) Phone   (c) Video call

My last text was to: _____

It said:

The last person I called: _____

We talked about: _____

Last photo/video in my camera roll: _____

My wallpaper right now: _____

My favorite game: _____

Last song I listened to: _____

Last podcast I listened to: _____

Next audiobook in my queue: _____

MY MOST USED EMOJI:

WHAT'S SOMETHING YOU BELIEVED ABOUT YOURSELF THAT WASN'T TRUE?

I stopped playing the saxophone in the eleventh grade, not because I didn't enjoy it, but because I didn't think I was good enough compared to the other musicians at my school. Years later, I still wish I had never stopped. Playing the saxophone is SO cool. There have been plenty of other times when I let self-doubt keep me from showing up and trying, but I've realized that the more I let that "not good enough" feeling dictate my decisions, the more I'm going to miss out on. Life goes by so quick—I don't want to let self-doubt steal another joyful moment or experience. And that's one of the reasons I started creating my own original music. I told myself for years I wasn't good enough to put my own stuff out there. Good enough for WHO, though? Now I'm finally starting to write songs that I love, and it never would've happened unless I'd pushed past that little voice in my head and accepted myself and my interests on my own terms. The reward has been so worth it.

Not smart enough. Not talented enough. Too loud. Too quiet. Too much. We've all allowed repeating messages of self-doubt to creep in at some point, somewhere along the way in our journeys. When we can recognize the source for what it is—fear—we can begin to embrace a new story about ourselves. A story where we recognize there's courage in just showing up, and that we've been enough for our own journey all along. What was a negative message you internalized about yourself when you were younger that isn't true? How did that belief limit you? What *is* true about you? What are your strengths? With what positive truth have you replaced that old lie? Write it down here.

_____

_____

_____

_____

_____

_____

_____

_____

_____

THIS OR THAT: MOVIE NIGHT

You're in charge of movie night.... What do you choose?

Movie at home	Go to the cinema
Rom-Com	Action
Comedy	Mystery
Thriller	Drama
Animated	Fantasy
Popcorn	Pretzel
Chocolate	Candy
Pizza	Hot Dog
Ice Cream	Cookies
Slushie	Soda

What are some movies on your "must see" list?

_____

_____

_____

_____

_____

_____

Share your answers on social media! #daybydayjournal

SELF CHECK-IN: MIND

Our minds are the hub for our overall well-being. Take a few minutes for a little mental check-in.

Date: _____

Right now my mind feels (circle): clear / fuzzy / tired / buzzing / calm / overwhelmed

What I'm most looking forward to today: _____

What I'm most worried about right now: _____

Biggest items on my to-do list today:

☐ _____

☐ _____

☐ _____

What I need to let go of/release control of: _____

One thing I can do to nourish my mind today: _____

One thing I can do to rest today: _____

Other things on my mind: _____

_____

_____

_____

_____

_____

_____

_____

PICKY EATER BINGO

Color in all the boxes with food items you don't like. If you fill in six in a row (vertically *or* horizontally), you might just have a picky palate. (It's okay, you're not alone!) On the other hand, if you leave an entire column or row blank, congrats—you just might be an adventurous eater!

MUSHROOMS	GREEN PEAS	BRUSSELS SPROUTS	ASPARAGUS	ONION	CAULIFLOWER
RAISINS	ALMOND BUTTER	PRUNES	CASHEWS	DARK CHOCOLATE	PISTACHIOS
LEMONADE	ORANGE JUICE	APPLE JUICE	COCONUT MILK	TEA	COFFEE
PICKLES	OLIVES	HUMMUS	KETCHUP	MUSTARD	MAYONNAISE
EGGS	TOFU	CHICKEN	FISH	BEEF	PORK
PINEAPPLE	TOMATO	BANANAS	MANGOES	KIWI	GRAPEFRUIT

Share your answers on social media! #daybydayjournal

WHAT IS YOUR FAVORITE OR FUNNIEST MEMORY FROM YOUR CHILDHOOD?

One of my favorite memories from childhood would definitely be the night I turned our family kitchen into a cooking show when I was about ten years old. The show was called Jess Just Cook. (Catchy, I know.) I made a three-course meal, starting with ham, cheese, and pineapple toasted sandwiches and ending with ice cream sundaes—a true chef in my gingerbread-man apron and matching chef's hat. The sweetest part of my cooking show debut was really that it was a full family affair. I made my mum and little brother, Toby, be the live audience. And my older sister, Sarah, was my "assistant." When watching the video (Dad videotaped everything back then!), you can tell my sister did NOT want to be there, but she was being a good sport for my enjoyment as good big sisters do. I don't know how my parents were able to keep a straight face the entire episode, but they definitely laugh about it now. And it's so much fun to remember those kinds of moments as a family with them today.

Write out your favorite or funniest memory from childhood below.

_____

_____

_____

_____

_____

_____

_____

_____

_____

_____

_____

_____

_____

_____

GOOD THINGS TAKE TIME

SELF CHECK-IN: BODY

//

Our bodies work so hard to take care of us. Let's take a quick pause to think about how we can better take care of them today too. Before answering the following questions, take a few slow, deep breaths.

Date: _____

Physically, I feel _____ today.

Does any part of my body hurt or ache?

YES (circle one) NO

If yes, what? _____

One thing I can do to care for my body today (e.g., stretch,

go for a walk, get a massage, make a green smoothie, etc.):

_____

Have I had enough water so far today? (Circle)

YES, I'm on track!   NO, I'll drink a glass right now.

My stress level right now is at a (circle):

0 1 2 3 4 5 6 7 8 9 10

What activities will I do to release stress from my body today?

_____

_____

What's something I can do today to set myself up for a good night's sleep later on?

_____

_____

Other than the above, how was my day?

_____

_____

UNPOPULAR OPINIONS

Wouldn't it be a boring world if we all thought the same way and liked the same things?
Circle YES or NO if you agree with these unpopular opinions.

Pineapple belongs on pizza.
YES / NO

Ketchup belongs in the fridge.
YES / NO

Nuts in chocolate are just wrong.
YES / NO

Showering at night is better than in the morning.
YES / NO

Cats are better than dogs.
YES / NO

Put milk in the bowl before cereal.
YES / NO

Calling is better than texting.
YES / NO

Orange juice tastes better with pulp.
YES / NO

Tomatoes ruin sandwiches.
YES / NO

An aisle seat on a plane is better than a window seat.
YES / NO

What's your own unpopular opinion?

_____

_____

Share your unpopular opinions on social media! #daybydayjournal

NEVER HAVE I EVER

///

Traveled overseas

I HAVE / I HAVE NEVER

If yes, when, where, and what was your favorite destination?

_____

Lied about my age

I HAVE / I HAVE NEVER

If yes, when and why?

_____

Been on TV

I HAVE / I HAVE NEVER

If yes, when and what for?

_____

Gotten a tattoo

I HAVE / I HAVE NEVER

If yes, when and what of?
How many?

_____

Gotten a piercing

I HAVE / I HAVE NEVER

If yes, where and how many?

_____

Had braces

I HAVE / I HAVE NEVER

If yes, for how long? What was your experience?

_____

Fallen in love

I HAVE / I HAVE NEVER

If yes, when and with whom?

_____

Gone skydiving

I HAVE / I HAVE NEVER

If yes, when and what was it like?

_____

Met a celebrity

I HAVE / I HAVE NEVER

If yes, when, who, and
what was your experience?

_____

Broken a bone

I HAVE / I HAVE NEVER

If yes, where and what happened?

_____

POSITIVE AFFIRMATIONS

The more we hear or see a repeated message about ourselves, the more we believe it. That's why giving ourselves positive affirmations is so important: because what we believe about ourselves becomes our reality. Write down some encouraging truths about yourself that you need to hear and see daily.

Examples: I am valued. I am trustworthy. I am good at what I do. I am a good listener. I am blessed with incredible friends.

Tip: Cut out your affirmations and place them in different spots where you'll see them daily (e.g., on the back of your phone case, on the refrigerator, on the bathroom mirror, etc.).

I am _____ I am _____

I am _____ I am _____

I am _____ I am _____

I am _____ I am _____

I am _____ I am _____

I am _____ I am _____

I am _____ I am _____

I am _____ I am _____

I am _____ I am _____

SELF CHECK-IN: HEART

//

Our emotions are external messengers for what's going on within. It's always worth the time to stop and listen to what they have to tell us and examine where we might need to give ourselves a little more TLC today.

Date: _____

In this moment, I feel _____ .

So far, the high point of today has been:

_____

So far, the low point of today has been:

_____

Something that has been on my heart recently:

_____

Something I can do to feel more at peace or give myself space today:

_____

Someone I want to reach out to/connect with today:

_____

At the moment, something I'm learning about myself is:

_____

Other things on my heart:

_____

_____

_____

_____

BRAIN DUMP

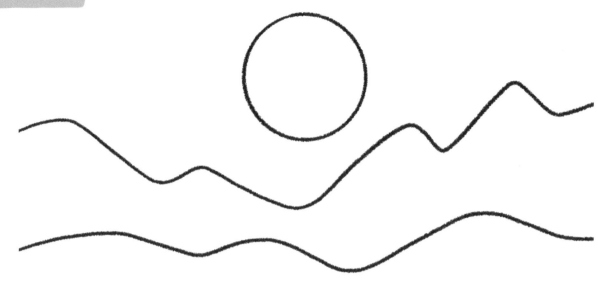

"WHEN YOU DO SOMETHING
BEAUTIFUL AND NOBODY NOTICES,
DO NOT BE SAD.

FOR THE SUN EVERY MORNING
IS A BEAUTIFUL SPECTACLE
AND YET MOST OF THE AUDIENCE
STILL SLEEPS."

– john lennon

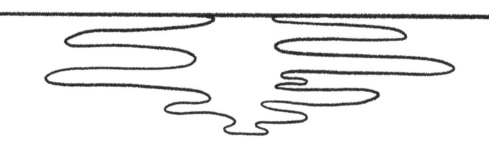

I WOULDN'T BE ME WITHOUT...

Relationships and experiences can shape our lives in such a profound way that it can be hard to describe in words. Fill this spread with photos of people, places, or things that complete the sentence "I wouldn't be me without..." And let yourself be encouraged by the "bigger picture" of what you see when the collage is complete.

WHAT'S THE HARDEST THING YOU'VE EVER DONE? AND HOW DID YOU GET THROUGH IT?

Look back on the most challenging situation or stretching season in your life. Maybe it was a challenge you chose to take on—like running your first marathon or studying for a degree while working full-time. Or maybe the difficulty happened to you by no choice of your own, but still, you had to push through it. What was it that made those circumstances so difficult? Where did you find the strength to keep going, and how did you overcome it?

_____

_____

_____

_____

_____

_____

_____

_____

_____

_____

_____

_____

_____

_____

_____

_____

_____

_____

_____

SELF CHECK-IN: MIND

Our minds are the hub for our overall well-being. Take a few minutes for a little mental check-in.

Date: _____

Right now my mind feels (circle): clear / fuzzy / tired / buzzing / calm / overwhelmed

What I'm most looking forward to today: _____

What I'm most worried about right now: _____

Biggest items on my to-do list today:

☐ _____

☐ _____

☐ _____

What I need to let go of/release control of: _____

One thing I can do to nourish my mind today: _____

One thing I can do to rest today: _____

Other things on my mind: _____

_____

_____

_____

_____

_____

_____

_____

MY FIRSTS

Our "firsts" tend to be memorable. Add as much detail as you can to the list of firsts below—the year, where you were, what you did, or whatever you remember!

My first friend:

_____

My first pet:

_____

My first house:

_____

My first crush:

_____

My first kiss:

_____

My first piercing:

_____

My first concert:

_____

My first phone:

_____

My first car:

_____

My first job:

_____

HAVE YOU EVER HAD A BROKEN HEART OR GONE THROUGH A BREAKUP?

Even if you have never gone through a breakup, most of us have experienced the pain of a broken heart in some way. Maybe you felt deeply vulnerable, as if the wound would never heal. Maybe you still feel that way. Use this space to process your experience, how it made you feel, and how you're feeling about it now. What have you learned about yourself through the heart-break? What are some ways you can invest in yourself and your well-being? What is something you need to hear from yourself to keep moving forward?

_____

_____

_____

_____

_____

_____

_____

_____

_____

_____

_____

_____

_____

_____

_____

_____

"there are far, far better things ahead than any we leave behind."

c.s. lewis

SELF CHECK-IN: BODY

//

Our bodies work so hard to take care of us. Let's take a quick pause to think about how we can better take care of them today too. Before answering the following questions, take a few slow, deep breaths.

Date: _____

Physically, I feel _____ today.

Does any part of my body hurt or ache?

YES   (circle one)   **NO**

If yes, what? _____

One thing I can do to care for my body today (e.g., stretch,

go for a walk, get a massage, make a green smoothie, etc.):

_____

Have I had enough water so far today? (Circle)

YES, I'm on track!   **NO, I'll drink a glass right now.**

My stress level right now is at a (circle):

0   1   2   3   4   5   6   7   8   9   10

What activities will I do to release stress from my body today?

_____

_____

What's something I can do today to set myself up for a good night's sleep later on?

_____

_____

Other than the above, how was my day?

_____

_____

WHO'S MOST LIKELY TO...

Pick a group of people in your life—it could be your family, closest friends, classmates, or coworkers—and fill in the blanks. Who is most likely to...

Become an actor?

_____

Become the CEO of a big company?

_____

Become a YouTuber?

_____

Forget important birthdays/anniversaries?

_____

Marry a celebrity?

_____

Be a stand-up comedian?

_____

Spoil a surprise?

_____

Move to a different country?

_____

Go to sleep the latest?

_____

Get a tattoo spontaneously?

_____

Share your answers on social media at #daybydayjournal and tag the people you mentioned!

ACTS OF KINDNESS CHALLENGE

I love the surprise element of random acts of kindness. Even when I'm not around to see the joy on the recipient's face, just knowing that I may have made their day in a small way makes mine. I know it'll make yours too.

See how many random acts of kindness you can check off in the next few weeks—and add your own. It's going to be so much fun!

☐ Bake for someone.

☐ Surprise someone with flowers.

☐ Hold the door open for someone.

☐ Pay for the person behind you in line (coffee shop, grocery store, etc.).

☐ Cook dinner for someone and invite them over or deliver it to their doorstep.

☐ Compliment a stranger.

☐ Spark friendly conversation with someone who serves you (waitress, cashier, etc.).

☐ Leave a note on the mirror or refrigerator for someone in your household saying you're thankful for them and why.

☐ Send a text of encouragement to a friend or family member.

☐ Help someone elderly when you're out in public (reaching a high shelf or lifting something heavy in the grocery store, etc.).

☐ Offer to babysit, free of charge, for a friend so they can go on a date with their partner.

☐ Leave an extra-generous tip with a "thank you" on the receipt.

☐ Put change in a vending machine.

☐ _____

☐ _____

☐ _____

☐ _____

important reminders:

take care of yourself. get plenty of sleep. be kind.

SELF CHECK-IN: HEART

//

Our emotions are external messengers for what's going on within. It's always worth the time to stop and listen to what they have to tell us and examine where we might need to give ourselves a little more TLC today.

Date: _____

In this moment, I feel _____ .

So far, the high point of today has been:

_____

So far, the low point of today has been:

_____

Something that has been on my heart recently:

_____

Something I can do to feel more at peace or give myself space today:

_____

Someone I want to reach out to/connect with today:

_____

At the moment, something I'm learning about myself is:

_____

Other things on my heart:

_____

_____

_____

_____

AD-LIBS

Ad-Libs are a fun way to pass the time with a friend or just by yourself. Fill in the blanks below with the correct type of word (a noun, adjective, or verb, etc.) and then use the list of words you selected to fill in the blanks next to the corresponding numbers in the story below. Try not to read the story until you've written in all of your words. It's more fun that way!

Write words for the following:

1. Time: _____

2. Verb: _____

3. Verb: _____

4. Person's name: _____

5. Noun: _____

6. Movement verb (e.g., skip): _____

7. Type of food (plural): _____

8. Adjective: _____

9. Song and artist: _____

10. Adjective: _____

11. Brand: _____

12. Smell or flavor: _____

13. Type of food: _____

14. Strange hobby: _____

STORY: MY MORNING ROUTINE

I usually wake up around (1. _____), and the first thing I have to do when I get

out of bed is (2. _____). I also have to (3. _____) before I can

do anything else. I usually check my phone to see if I have any missed calls or texts. Most of the

time it's (4. _____) asking about my (5. _____).

I (6. _____) downstairs to make myself some breakfast. I always have

(7. _____). It's just so, so (8. _____). When it's time to

shower, I like to turn on (9. _____ by _____)...it always puts

me in a (10. _____) mood. I use my favorite (11. _____)

(12. _____)-scented body wash before using my (13. _____)-scented

shampoo and conditioner. Lastly, before I get started with the rest of my day, I do like to

(14. _____)...it's my guilty pleasure!

WRITE A LETTER TO: YOUR FUTURE SELF

Reflecting on what you would want your future self to know about your life right now is a great way to check in—to remind yourself of who you are, how far you've come, and how you want to live moving forward. Use this letter to help you define what is most important and meaningful to you in this season of life. What could you never live without? What do you feel proud of? What are you worried about? What do you never want to forget about your life right now? How would you like to see yourself grow?

Dear _____ -Year-Old Me,

_____

_____

_____

_____

_____

_____

_____

_____

_____

_____

_____

_____

_____

_____

_____

_____

_____

_____

_____

_____

HAND LETTERING

You don't have to be an expert at calligraphy to enjoy trying or practicing hand lettering. Trace the letters below, and enjoy the slow, fluid movement of creating art with words.

Tip: A brush pen or pen art markers are best for hand lettering, but if you don't have those on hand, any pen will do!

love love

joy joy

peace peace

copy copy

sun sun

ocean ocean

LOVE LANGUAGES

(Read *The Five Love Languages* by Gary Chapman!)

It has made such a difference in my relationships to understand how those closest to me want to be loved, instead of assuming that they all prefer to receive love the same way I do. For example, I feel most loved when someone gives me quality time. I adore being able to sit with someone with our phones put away, giving each other our full attention and really feeling connected in our shared time together. For my husband, Gabriel, on the other hand, quality time is quite low on his list, and receiving words of encouragement is at the top. Without that awareness, I could be trying my best to love Gabriel by giving him my full time and attention, yet what he really needs is words—to be told how much I love him, why I'm proud of him, and so on. One year for Gabriel's birthday, I created a heart out of Post-it Notes on his bathroom mirror with a different thing I love about him written on each Post-it. Such a simple thing, but because I was speaking his love language, to Gabriel it was huge.

What makes you feel most loved? Have you ever identified your primary love language— the way you best receive love? Is it...

☐ Quality Time

☐ Physical Affection

☐ Words of Encouragement

☐ Being Heard (really listened to)

☐ Receiving Presents

☐ Thoughtful Surprises/Spontaneity

☐ Other: _____

Because everyone experiences love differently, knowing your own love language and that of those around you can be a game-changer when it comes to really showing you care, better communicating your own needs, and generally growing closer in your relationships.
What are some examples of ways you feel most loved by others?

_____

_____

_____

_____

What are the love languages of some of your closest relationships? Ask a few people around you (family members, best friend, etc.) how they best receive love and record their answers below.

Name: _____

Their primary way of receiving love: _____

How can you be practicing this love language with them? _____

_____

_____

_____

Name: _____

Their primary way of receiving love: _____

How can you be practicing this love language with them?   _____

_____

_____

_____

Name: _____

Their primary way of receiving love: _____

How can you be practicing this love language with them? _____

_____

_____

_____

SELF CHECK-IN: MIND

Our minds are the hub for our overall well-being. Take a few minutes for a little mental check-in.

Date: _____

Right now my mind feels (circle): clear / fuzzy / tired / buzzing / calm / overwhelmed

What I'm most looking forward to today: _____

What I'm most worried about right now: _____

Biggest items on my to-do list today:

☐ _____

☐ _____

☐ _____

What I need to let go of/release control of: _____

One thing I can do to nourish my mind today: _____

One thing I can do to rest today: _____

Other things on my mind: _____

_____

_____

_____

_____

_____

_____

_____

"DON'T LOOK BACK.
YOU'RE NOT GOING THAT WAY."

THE STRANGEST THING I EVER...

The answers to these kinds of questions always make for the best (and funniest) stories. Fill in as many as apply to you!

Strangest thing I've ever eaten:

_____

Strangest injury I've ever had:

_____

Strangest trend I've ever tried:

_____

Strangest date I've ever been on:

_____

Strangest reason I got in trouble at school:

_____

Strangest encounter with a stranger:

_____

Strangest place I've ever had to change clothes:

_____

Strangest beauty technique I've tried:

_____

Strangest talent I have:

_____

Strangest experience I've had in a taxi or on public transportation:

_____

A SENSE OF HOME

//

Think of a home in your past that holds the best memories for you. Maybe it's your childhood home, a grandparent's house where you spent lots of time, or even your first apartment living on your own. Let these questions bring back to mind the details of a special place that will always feel like home, even if it's just in your memories and heart.

What home did you pick to write about, and why? _____

_____

Who lived in this home? _____

_____

What did it look like on the outside? _____

What was your favorite room? Why? _____

_____

What details can you remember about your favorite room? What did the wall color and flooring look like? What did it smell like? What was your favorite piece of furniture and favorite thing to do there? _____

_____

_____

Describe a vivid, happy memory you have from your time in this home. _____

_____

What was your favorite meal to eat there? _____

What was your favorite holiday to celebrate there? Who would come? _____

_____

If this home were a person, how would you describe its personality? _____

_____

What do you miss most about being there? _____

_____

My experiences (and years of apartment living) have taught me that you don't have to wait until you can acquire your "dream home" to create calm, happy living spaces. Start small: Bring in some potted plants or arrange an open shelf with things that make you feel good when you see them. Keep your eyes peeled for simple design ideas that you want to try, but don't worry about keeping up with the trends. Your spaces should be an expression of yourself and what makes you unique, and most importantly, what makes you feel at home.

No matter what season of life or type of home you're in now, it's always fun to dream about designing living spaces that will inspire and nurture you in the future. What kind of ambience do you want to create in your home? Use this space to sketch or place printouts of home-design details and features (wall colors or paper, shelving, furniture, finishes, etc.) that light you up and make you excited for your home now and in the future.

DREAM HOME STYLE BOARD

SELF CHECK-IN: BODY

//

Our bodies work so hard to take care of us. Let's take a quick pause to think about how we can better take care of them today too. Before answering the following questions, take a few slow, deep breaths.

Date: _____

Physically, I feel _____ today.

Does any part of my body hurt or ache?

YES   (circle one)   NO

If yes, what? _____

One thing I can do to care for my body today (e.g., stretch,

go for a walk, get a massage, make a green smoothie, etc.):

_____

Have I had enough water so far today? (Circle)

YES, I'm on track!   NO, I'll drink a glass right now.

My stress level right now is at a (circle):

0   1   2   3   4   5   6   7   8   9   10

What activities will I do to release stress from my body today?

_____

_____

What's something I can do today to set myself up for a good night's sleep later on?

_____

_____

Other than the above, how was my day?

_____

_____

1 - LIGHT BLUE   2 - ORANGE   3 - DARK GREEN
4 - LIGHT GREEN   5 - PINK   6 - YELLOW

WHAT ARE YOU EXCITED ABOUT FOR THE FUTURE?

Every once in a while, I like to sit down and just dream on paper about the future. I wonder about how my work will evolve creatively or how much my husband and I will have grown together. I think about what it will be like to become parents one day and what an incredible journey that will be. Letting myself get excited for good things ahead—even if they end up looking way different than I imagined—always gives me a bit more inspiration for what's right in front of me today.

Let yourself daydream about the things you most look forward to in the years ahead. What would your life look like if all your hopes and aspirations came to be?

_____

_____

_____

_____

_____

_____

_____

_____

_____

_____

_____

_____

_____

_____

_____

_____

_____

NOTICING SOMETHING IN A NEW WAY

Slowing down allows us to really see things we've never taken the time to notice before, though they may have been right in front of us all along. Whether you're outside or in, take a look around. What catches your eye? Is it how ivy cascades down the wall? The way the light streams through the window? A book with a beautiful cover? Draw something that captures your interest that you may have previously overlooked, and take a moment to appreciate what it adds to your world in this moment.

TOUGH TIMES NEVER LAST,

BUT TOUGH PEOPLE DO.

robert h. schuller

SELF CHECK-IN: HEART

//

Our emotions are external messengers for what's going on within. It's always worth the time to stop and listen to what they have to tell us and examine where we might need to give ourselves a little more TLC today.

Date: _____

In this moment, I feel _____ .

So far, the high point of today has been:

_____

So far, the low point of today has been:

_____

Something that has been on my heart recently:

_____

Something I can do to feel more at peace or give myself space today:

_____

Someone I want to reach out to/connect with today:

_____

At the moment, something I'm learning about myself is:

_____

Other things on my heart:

_____

_____

_____

_____

WRITE A LETTER TO: SOMEONE YOU LOVE

If tomorrow never came, what would you want to make sure you told someone you love?

Dear: _____

_____

_____

_____

_____

_____

_____

_____

_____

_____

_____

_____

_____

_____

_____

_____

_____

_____

_____

_____

_____

Don't wait until it's too late! Call them (or cut out your letter and mail it) today.

TIME WELL SPENT

//

At the very beginning of *Day by Day*, you wrote a letter to yourself, setting your intention for using this journal and stating what you wanted to get out of it.

 Now write a letter to yourself reflecting on those same questions (in the past tense). What did time spent journaling—and switching off the noise around you—bring to your life? What's happening in your life now? How are you really feeling about it all? What has taking more time to focus on yourself meant for your well-being?

Date: _____

_____

_____

_____

_____

_____

_____

_____

_____

_____

_____

Now flip back and read your very first journal entry. How does this letter compare?

_____

_____

_____

_____

_____

AUTHOR'S NOTE

I'm so honored that you took the time to complete this journal and go on this little journey with me. I hope you found joy and peace in these little quiet moments spent away from your phone and the busyness of your world. And I hope you discovered that any "me time" taken to invest in your own well-being is always time well spent.

God bless,
Jess Conte

ABOUT THE AUTHOR

Jess Conte is a lover of stationery, journaling, interior design, graphic design, music, and creating content. She is a YouTube star and a social media influencer. She is also a music artist from Australia, but she now lives in Florida with her husband. She is a talented graphic design artist and also features photos of her artistic skill on Instagram. She and her husband met in 2016 and married after they bonded over faith and music.

Copyright © 2023 by Jess Conte

Cover design by Gabriella Wikidal. Cover images by Elle Suko.
Cover copyright © 2023 by Hachette Book Group, Inc.

Hachette Book Group supports the right to free expression and the value
of copyright. The purpose of copyright is to encourage writers and artists to
produce the creative works that enrich our culture.

The scanning, uploading, and distribution of this book without permission is
a theft of the author's intellectual property. If you would like permission to
use material from the book (other than for review purposes), please contact
permissions@hbgusa.com. Thank you for your support of the author's rights.

Ellie Claire
Worthy
Hachette Book Group
1290 Avenue of the Americas, New York, NY 10104
worthypublishing.com
twitter.com/worthypub

First Edition: January 2023

Ellie Claire and Worthy are divisions of Hachette Book Group, Inc. The Ellie
Claire name and logo are trademarks of Hachette Book Group, Inc.

The publisher is not responsible for websites (or their content) that are not
owned by the publisher.

The Hachette Speakers Bureau provides a wide range of authors for speaking
events. To find out more, go to www.hachettespeakersbureau.com or
call (866) 376-6591.

ISBN: 978-1-5460-1594-9 (paper over board)

Printed in Spain

EP

10 9 8 7 6 5 4 3 2